Table of Content

YOUR GIFT

I wanted to show my appreciation that you support my work so I've put together a free gift for you.

http://bonusfreebook.org/

Just visit the link above to download it now.

I know you will love this gift.

Thank you for attention!
With love,
John Thornton

INTRODUCTION

You have probably heard about the Atkins Diet, but do you know that much about it? You might also have a negative mindset towards this diet, having heard rumors about it in the past, but the bottom line is that everything changes over time, and that includes the Atkins Diet.

Put simply, the Atkins diet is a very effective and easy to follow, one which gives you guaranteed, effective results, and also helps you learn and recognize healthy food habits which will change your outlook on dietary nutrition for life.

No counting, no red or green days, and nothing too complicated in the slightest.

If you have picked up this book then you are no doubt very interested in following the Atkins Diet, and you have probably already learned a little about it to start with. At first, we will reiterate the diet's history, how it works, how to follow it, and also quickly run through the phases and what you need to do in each one. After that, we will get onto the practical stuff, the recipes!

The aim of this book is to show you that the Atkins Diet gives you endless choice and freedom when it comes to delicious meals and snacks. You don't have to be a super chef to be able to follow this diet, and you don't need to spend a fortune on expensive Ingredients – many Ingredients for this diet are already in your fridge, freezer, or kitchen cupboards.

So, let's get onto the mechanics of the diet, before moving onto the recipes themselves.

WHAT IS THE ATKINS DIET?

Derived from a best-selling book written in 1972 by cardiologist Dr. Robert Atkins, the Atkins diet is what is generally referred to as a low-carb diet. Although quite unpopular upon its first emergence due to increased fat intake, the Akins diet has gained increased popularity over the last decade. In this chapter, we will cover what the Atkins diet is, how it works, and how to use it to your advantage as a weight loss Method.

THE BASICS OF THE ATKINS DIET

The Atkins diet is a four-stage diet that focuses on losing weight by reducing carbohydrate consumption. This reduction in carbohydrate consumption results in more stable sugar levels in the body, as well as decreased hunger, fewer food cravings, and reduced fat storage.

So, how do these benefits come about from simply reducing carbohydrate consumption? Atkins focuses on the fact that the body is able to utilize two different types of food groups for energy – sugars (carbohydrates) and fats.

Most people are familiar with the concept of the body utilizing sugars for fuel. As the body breaks down carbohydrates, sugars are produced in the form of glucose. These sugars are then used to feed cells to provide the body with energy. The body prefers to feed on sugars first because they are easily accessible and easily broken down. When foods result in too much sugar being produced in the body, that excess sugar is stored as glycogen in the liver. However, when the liver can store no more glycogen the sugar is stored as fat throughout the body.

What many people are not familiar with is the fact that the body can also utilize fat for energy. When there is no easily accessible sugar (as found in carbohydrates) to break down for energy, the body will turn to fat. Breaking down fat will release stored sugars that can then be used for fuel. Breaking down the fat in your body for sugar will then result in weight loss as these fat cells are destroyed. This process of burning fat for energy is called "lipolysis." When lipolysis takes place and the existing stores of fat are burned, the body then releases something called ketones. By eating a diet that is low in carbohydrates, you are forcing your body into lipolysis. This process can be maintained by eating a diet that is high in fats, as it tricks your body into thinking that the fats that you are consuming are part of the natural process of lipolysis.

...But Isn't Eating a High Fat Diet Bad?

If you are like most people then you have had it drilled into your head that fats are bad. As it happens, when the Atkin's diet was first introduced it was met with considerable criticism over this very issue. Followers of the diet were worried that high fat intake would increase cholesterol and contribute to heart disease.

The Atkins diet does indeed incorporate higher fat intake, however, the fats that are recommended are saturated fats. It is true to say that the consumption of fats has gained a poor reputation over the past number of decades. It had been widely recognized that there was a direct link between fat intake and the risk of heart disease. However, current research has now shown that contrary to popular belief there is no solid evidence of any clear or definite link between heart disease and saturated fats. The British Medical Journal, amongst many reputable governing bodies and organizations, stated quite clearly in 2015 that they have found no link between saturated fats and the risks of strokes, coronary disease or type 2 diabetes.

Importantly for the Atkins Diet, the research does make a definite distinction between saturated fats and trans fats. The Atkins diet does promote the consumption of natural fats or saturated fats which are found in meats, salmon, dairy products and eggs. However, it would avoid trans fats which are found in long shelf life products such as snacks, packaged and processed foods, and margarine. Obviously, as with any food group, it is essential to maintain a balance with regards to the amount of fats being consumed. With this in mind, all phases of the Atkins diet will ensure that one will burn both the dietary and body fat for energy throughout the process.

We also need to consider that when one reduces the consumption of good fats it often tends to result in increased carbohydrate intake, as the body seeks to replace the old food source with a new one. This transfer back to consuming carbohydrates actually increases the chances of heart disease and unnecessary illnesses.

THE HISTORY OF THE ATKINS DIET

The Atkins Diet was originally known as the Atkins nutritional approach when it was first introduced. In these early years, fad diets were not as widespread as they are today. Calling it a nutritional approach truly exemplified what it was—an approach that provides nutrition and can change people's lives.

Dr. Robert C. Atkins began this nutritional approach based on a medical research paper he read in 1958. In his earliest books in the 1970's which introduced his diet said that the differentiating factor between the Atkins Diet and others is that the Atkins Diet will help people burn fat and consequently calories. People will be able to lose weight and keep the weight off, if they understood the basic principles of this low-carbohydrate plan.

The Atkins Diet focuses on an incorrect element in the standard American diet and its recommended food servings. For example, the Food Guide Pyramid suggests six to eleven servings per day of refined carbohydrates like bread, pasta, cereal, or rice, while stating that only three to five servings of vegetables and only two to three servings of proteins are needed in a person's diet. Dr. Atkins challenged this older belief, based on the failing health and increased weight levels of the patients he saw every day.

According to his book, Dr. Atkins' New Diet Revolution, he says that the trouble began when industry titans, government officials, and lobbyists started incorrectly influencing the public. There was a time where sugar was not discouraged much as it should have been. Low-fat messages were wrongly advocated in the 1980's and 1990's and it leads to the disastrous health of the majority of people today. Food companies responded to these trends by marketing fast, pre-packaged, and processed foods with "low-fat" or "fat-free," while adding addictive sugar or sugar substitute properties.

Prior to the Atkins Diet's introduction, many people assumed that wheat portions were an essential part of a healthy diet and that fats that came from olive oil or butter for example were the food elements to eliminate. This is because people thought a diet with any fat at all was bad. However, studies have shown how incorrect these principles were and are. Carbohydrates like bread and pasta offer no nutritional value. Healthy fats from protein like fish, nuts, or olive oil, can provide essential nutrients, leaving people feeling nourished and full of energy for the entire day.

Historically, Dr. Atkins was the first diet researcher to make these claims. He stated that a low-carb diet makes positive, fat burning changes to a person's metabolism. The Atkins Diet limits carbohydrates that do not provide energy or value. Many carbohydrates can negatively change a person's blood sugar level, causing severe problems later on down the road.

Additionally, Dr. Atkins proposed that a diet with servings of carbohydrates that equal or outdo servings of protein lead to hunger. This is why a low-fat diet (which essentially means high carbohydrates) does not work. People may lose weight quickly at first, but their hunger will cause problems like overeating. The body is also not designed to break down and digest carbohydrates as easily as proteins or fiber (found in vegetables).

In his books, he reiterates that a healthy, long-term, sustainable diet needs to possess healthy fats, protein, and fiber as its core components. Only then can people begin to lose weight and keep it off.

The history of the Atkins Diet stems from Dr. Atkins examination of sugar levels hidden in carbohydrates. Based on his work with patients and his examination of previously (and incorrectly) established government approved food serving guidelines, he determined that carbohydrates needed to be eliminated in order to promote health and increase weight loss.

In the Atkins nutritional approach, Dr. Atkins diet plan proposals are the still the same as the core principles of the diet now.

THE DIFFERENCE BETWEEN THE ATKINS DIET AND OTHER LOW-CARB DIETS

The reason why the Atkins Diet has lasted is simply that it is realistic, does not leave people hungry, and does not concentrate around deprivation.

Other low-carb diets have principles that mirror the essential components of the Atkins Diet, but may take on a more Mediterranean focus by including more fish and olive oil as daily food requirements.

In other variations of low-carb diets, people choose to cut all refined and processed carbs from their diets and consume only animal proteins, spices (for flavor), and related fats like oil. With zero carbs consumed, drastic weight loss and a return to a healthy metabolism results. However, this variation of a low-carb diet has an absence of essential vitamins and nutrient rich properties found in fruits and vegetables. For people who were obese or had serious health issues, the quick and immediate elimination of all carbs may be too drastic. This may result in overeating at a later time. A gradual lessening of all refined carbohydrates is ideal. This will prevent yo-yo dieting and can better result in lasting change.

THE SCIENCE BEHIND THE ATKINS DIET: WHY IT WORKS

The Atkins Diet works and has lasted in popular culture's realm because of the word-of mouth results and its practical principles. The science behind the Atkins diet focuses on carbohydrates and addictive sugar and flour.

Understanding the dangers of excessive sugar is an important component for losing weight, keeping it off, and maintaining high levels of above-average health. High blood sugar levels are severely problematic if sustained, because the body cannot digest processed foods (like pasta), that are not found in nature. A pasta tree does not exist! And your body is a natural entity. It will have a difficult time breaking down something so unnatural, factory created, and highly processed. Over time, this leads to weight gain and a sometimes, permanent metabolic change. It will become difficult to not only lose the weight, but it will be hard to fight off the cravings caused by the addictive flavors and properties found in starchy, non-nutritional food, like pasta, cookies, or cereal.

Dr. Atkins' extensive patient work and research through the years led him to examine insulin and its dangerous levels in his patients. Based on this, he proposed that the carbohydrates people were consuming in a standard American diet were (and still are) very harmful. This is because it produces high levels of glucose in people.

The types of carbohydrates consumed will definitely have an effect on blood sugar levels. This can be positive or negative. In a standard Northern American diet, foods filled with flour and processed, refined sugar properties are common. There is high fructose corn syrup in almost everything. From store-bought salad dressings to pre-packaged, refined sugar and flour, sandwiches and cookies are everywhere.

Dr. Atkins centered the development of this diet in part on the science and examination of rising blood sugar levels in people. Insulin brings glucose through your blood and moves it until it hits your cells. However, as sugar levels rise, it cannot be converted into energy due to the refined nature of the carbohydrates. So, your body stores that unneeded, excess glucose as fat. This is exemplified physically through visible weight gain and physical transformations like: beer bellies, "love handles", and cellulite pockets on the belly, hips, buttocks, thighs, and other parts of the leg region.

Excess glucose from refined carbohydrates produces excess fat. And while, you may have mistakenly believed that a low-fat diet is needed, you were misguided. The main culprit in preventable diseases like heart disease, stroke, and diabetes is sugar.

A high level of carbohydrate consumption which is common today results in high blood sugar levels. When insulin is overproduced, energy is not properly converted. This leads to common experiences that you may have felt like midday sleepiness, the inability to focus at school or work, or other ailments that affect your ability to be productive or fully present during the day.

Carbohydrate food staples like mashed potatoes, sugar, cream, or French fries, are common in Northern American diets. The dangerous downside is that they can quickly convert to high levels of glucose. And based on the food pyramid, people are following its guidelines, even though they are harmful to them. Higher consumption levels of vegetables and nutrient-rich proteins are better for blood sugar levels and your overall health.

An overweight or obese person has already experienced negative changes to their metabolism. Their insulin ability may not be effective and so their body starts storing excess glucose, which is fat. When insulin becomes excessive it leads to severe health risks like obesity. This level of insulin can cause a person to have no energy, excessive fat, and physical limitations.

Another result is that you will need more and more refined carbohydrates. Your body will become used to those foods and it will be what you crave. This is due to metabolic changes, physical routines, and the addictive chemical properties found in refined carbohydrates, processed food and desserts, and nearly all packaged food items that fill the grocery store aisles today.

In his scientific research findings, Dr. Atkins talks about the health issues that result from improper insulin levels. According to his book, Dr. Atkins states numerous times that the process of excess blood glucose will lead to an overproduction of what your body needs. In many people, especially those who consume unnaturally, processed carbohydrates, may have a higher chance of developing hyperinsulinism and consequently diabetes. Obesity, breast cancer, and heart disease (which is a leading killer) are completely preventable through maintaining a healthy weight and limiting refined carbohydrate ridden foods.

The scientific connection between life-threatening illnesses and insulin abnormalities is a trend that Dr. Atkins noticed was rising. Now diabetes and other related diseases are a pervasive part of our societies. This is due to multiple factors like an incorrect food serving suggestion guide as well as the introduction and spread of fast food outlets and chains.

Science data shows that cardiovascular diseases are definitely connected to insulin resistance and excessive glucose in the blood and body. Heart disease is the leading cause of death. For most people, this is entirely preventable through lifestyle and dietary changes. These dietary changes need to be lasting, effective, and rational. And the Atkins' Diet will help you make these vital changes in your life. The best course of action for your mind, body, and overall health can be achieved through the healthy ways of the Atkins Diet.

HOW TO PREPARE FOR THE ATKINS DIET

The first way to prepare for the Atkins Diet (aside from reading this starter guide of course!) is to understand that continued consumption of excessive refined carbohydrates will make it difficult to lose weight. If you crave them after a long day of work, late at night, or when you are going through a stressful period, it is best not to have them in the house. There is no nutritional value in flour or sugar. Do not buy these food products. Do not keep them in your house. You are one step closer to fully adopting the Atkins Diet, by eradicating your home access to carbohydrates.

Secondly, you need to understand that fad diets that include low-fat suggestions are not good for you and do not align with the Atkins Diet in any way. Fat won't cause abnormalities and disruptions to your glucose or insulin. Rather, it will help you feel full when you consume whole, healthy proteins. On the Atkins Diet, you will be eating the right amounts and you won't be hungry throughout the day like when you consume refined carbohydrates. For example, healthy fats from fish will nourish your body with omega-3 and other fatty acids. These properties can help stave off certain diseases when consumed in alignment with the complete Atkins Diet.

You may think that you do not have the willpower to resist certain foods or that you do not have the strength to skip snacking, which was most likely part of your old (unhealthy) routine. But be prepared for the positive changes! Once you start and stick with the Atkins Diet, you will only eat full meals full or nutrient rich foods. Your body will use your fat and burn it. You will realize that you won't be hungry because your food is being properly allocated where it is needed...as energetic fuel.

Be prepared to stop counting calories. The Atkins Diet can help you lose weight and improve your health by guiding with you with food choices that are healthy and filling. Counting calories or total deprivation is not a sustainable eating plan or way of life. The Atkins Diet is.

If you adopt the Atkins Diet be prepared to choose certain food groups. This is needed because as you will learn and as we will discuss later on in this guide, natural, unprocessed carbohydrates may be allowed to be part of your diet. It is crucial to prepare and understand the differentiating factors between certain food groups that the Atkins Diet encourages you to have. You also have to be prepared to pay attention to your body and what it responds to.

For instance, fiber can be considered a carbohydrate in some cases. And it can be a part of your diet, because it is good for you. Fiber absorbs toxic elements in the body, acts as a natural diuretic, improves the immune system, and rids the body of bad cholesterol, to name a few. Fiber can be found in fruits, vegetables, nuts, and unprocessed grains. At the start of the Atkins Diet, may encourage the consumption of vegetables only, until you are used to eating them regularly. Then, the introduction of other sources of fiber will be helpful to give yourself a diet that is well rounded and pleasing.

The Atkins Diet was created and exists as a form of natural healthcare, renewal, and change. However, if you are overweight, have suffered from serious health problems (or are still suffering from them), or are obese, it is important to always consult a doctor prior to beginning this nutritional approach.

MEDICAL AWARENESS

For those who are starting this diet as a response to their current poor state of health or physical limitations, there is much to be proud of. You have made a decision. You have done your research. You have decided that the Atkins Diet sounds like rational and realistic possibility for you to adopt, in order to change. However, there are still medical facets to consider in relation to your current state of health or to any illnesses you may be suffering from.

- It is important to continue taking any diabetes injections or heart medications. The Atkins' Diet can help you begin to change your health, but you still need to be aware of your current health issues and address those problems by taking your prescribed medication.

- Consult your physician and let him or her know that you are starting the Atkins' Diet. If they have any additional instructions about the diet or your medication, follow their advice. Listen to their guidance. They will be proud of you for taking a proactive first step towards change. Additionally, any doctor will tell you that cutting refined sugar in carbohydrates is a great step.

- While consulting your physician you should also get a complete and thorough physical, along with any other applicable tests, as well as blood work. Once you have implemented the Atkins Diet in your life, looking back at your physical will be a starting point. You will proudly be able to see how far you've come.

- After you have committed and begun the Atkins Diet, you and your doctor will have to pay close attention to any effects that your medication has your blood sugar levels decreasing due to the Atkins Diet. The quantity or dosage may need to change, based on their decision.

- Communicate closely and regularly with your medical doctor, especially if you currently have or did suffer from any physical health disease.

ADVANTAGES OF THE ATKINS DIET

The Atkins Diet is still around years after Dr. Atkins first presented his research and wrote several best-selling books, because the Atkins Diet provides sustainable results and a healthy lifestyle change - plain and simple.

While the thought of giving up your previous diet of delicious tasting (unhealthy) snacks and foods may seem daunting, it is important to remember the advantages of the Atkins Diet. For one, the Atkins Diet results in positive metabolic change, which will allow you to burn fat, lose weight, and feel good about yourself. It is a realistic change that can be a permanent part of your life.

The Atkins Diet will stabilize your blood sugar. This is crucial in order to have fewer cravings and binges. It is incredibly beneficial to only consume healthy spaced out meals at appropriate times. The Atkins Diet principles will help you eliminate useless snacking throughout the day.

Some of the advantages to the Atkins Diet are the health benefits. The foods that this diet encourages are incredibly nutrient rich, natural, and unprocessed. Lean meat, fish, eggs, and whole vegetables, to name a few, energize the body. Millions of years ago, people ate the same natural foods from the ground and sea, and had no presence of the modern heart diseases of today.

The Atkins Diet will give health and energy advantages in your life. You will not be eating empty calories but rather, satisfying, tasty food. It may be a diet plan, but it is not a deprivation filled diet. There are many advantages and a lot to look forward too. Your new body, your new mind, and your new outlook are steps away. Keep reading to learn more about what's coming up.

BAKED MEATBALLS

Cooking time: Half an hour

Recipe makes 4 servings

Total carbs per serving 1.8g

Ingredients

- Extra virgin olive oil, 1 tablespoon
- Spring onion
- Garlic, 1.5 teaspoons
- Ground veal, 0.5lb
- Ground beef, 0.5lb
- Ground pork, 0.5lb
- Grated parmesan cheese, 0.5 cup
- 2 large eggs
- Salt, 0.5 teaspoon
- Black pepper, 0.25 teaspoon

Method

1. Preheat the oven to 190°C
2. Cook the onion until soft.
3. Add the garlic to the onion and cook for one-minute extra
4. In a large bowl, combine the veal, beef, and pork
5. Add the rest of the Ingredients to the bowl and mix well
6. Roll into small meatballs and place on a baking tray
7. Bake in the oven for 25 minutes, until cooked

Tips & Tricks/Did You Know?

You might have this particular dish down as a dinner recipe, but it is actually a breakfast dish, which goes very well to start your day! The filling nature of this dish will keep you full and also works a part of your protein intake.

Cooking time: Less than 5 minutes

Recipe makes 4 servings

Total carbs per serving - 2.4g

Ingredients

- Boiled eggs, around 8
- Full mayonnaise, 0.5 cup
- Dijon mustard, 3 tablespoons
- Salt, 0.5 teaspoon
- black pepper, 0.25 teaspoon
- Celery stalks, around 2 will be enough

Method

1. Boil the eggs as usual, to your liking
2. Chop the boiled eggs up into rough or small pieces, depending on how you like them
3. Mix the eggs together with the mayonnaise, mustard, salt and pepper
4. Combine well.
5. Chop up the celery into small pieces and add to the mixture
6. You can now serve the mixture; lettuce will be a good serving bed.

Tips & Tricks/Did You Know?

This particular dish is not only for phase 1 because you can have this at any phase and add in low carb bread or a tortilla, as you add more carbs to your diet in the next few phases. Remember to adjust the carb amount by doing this.

Cooking time: Less than 5 minutes

Recipe makes 6 servings

Total carbs per serving 3.2g

Ingredients

- Asparagus spears, around 30 in total
- Sun-dried tomatoes, 1.5oz
- balsamic vinegar, 1 tablespoon
- red wine vinegar, 1 tablespoon
- Garlic – ¼ teaspoon
- extra virgin olive oil, 3 tablespoons

Method

1. Place the asparagus in a steamer, or place over a steaming pot of boiling water for around 4 minutes, covered over. Ensure the asparagus is tender and green before removing from the heat.
2. Add the rest of the Ingredients to a blender and combine.
3. Add salt and pepper to taste
4. Drizzle on top of the asparagus and serve

Tips & Tricks/Did You Know?

To ensure the asparagus is properly cooked, you should let it stay on the heat until it is bright green and tender, not at all crispy. Red wine vinegar is also best as it is less acidic than regular vinegar, and works very well with the balsamic for an extra luxurious taste!

Cooking time: Half an hour

Recipe makes 6 servings

Total carbs per serving 1.4g

Ingredients

- Choose between bacon, ham, or sausage, 1lb of either, broken into small pieces
- Shredded cheese, 8oz
- 4 eggs
- Heavy cream, 1.5 cups

Method

1. Preheat the oven to 200°C
2. Take a large muffin tray and spray it with non-stick spray
3. Divide the meat into each muffin tray section
4. Add cheese equally to each section
5. In a bowl, mix together the eggs and heavy cream
6. Pour this mixture into each section
7. Bake for half an hour, until golden and spongy

Tips & Tricks/Did You Know?

If you're looking for a bakery-style treat in the morning, or perhaps a snack or lunch time picks me up, this is an ideal dish to try. Bake them in the morning or the night before, let them cool and store them in a plastic tub, taking them to work with you, and getting you through the day.

Cooking time: 20 minutes

Recipe makes 6 servings

Total carbs per serving 8.5g

Ingredients

- 3 large broccolis, chopped
- 2 large cauliflowers, chopped
- Jar of pimentos, 2 tablespoons
- Half a yellow bell pepper, chopped

- Ricotta cheese, 0.5 cup
- Nonfat cottage cheese, 1 cup
- Shredded cheddar, 1 cup
- Skimmed mozzarella, shredded, 3oz

Method

1. Preheat the oven to 160°C
2. In a large bowl, combine all Ingredients.
3. Take a casserole dish/pan and spray with non-stick spray, place the mixture inside the dish/pan
4. Bake in the oven for 15 minutes

Tips & Tricks/Did You Know?

The high fat content of this dish is ideal for the first phase of the Atkins diet, and this is also one of the most filling dishes you can have. This particular dish is ideal for an evening meal, and will also give you a good protein hit - 15.2g per serving.

Cooking time: Half an hour

Recipe makes 2 servings

Total carbs per serving 13.4g

Ingredients

- Brussel sprouts, around 10
- Brown mushrooms, 6oz
- Olive oil, 2 tablespoons
- Thyme, 2 teaspoons
- Paprika, 1 teaspoon
- Cinnamon, 1/8 teaspoon
- Garlic, 2 cloves

- Ground beef, 14 oz
- Chili powder, 1 tablespoon
- Salt, 1 teaspoon
- Black pepper, 0.5 teaspoon
- Tomato paste, 2 tablespoons
- Sour cream, 0.25 cup

Method

1. Place a pot of water on the stove and bring it to a boil
2. Cut the Brussel sprouts in half and add them to the boiling water
3. Over medium heat, add the oil to a skillet pan and allow to warm up
4. Chop up the mushrooms whilst the pan is heating up
5. Add the mushrooms to the pan and cook for just over 5 minutes, until brown
6. To the pan, add the thyme, paprika, cinnamon, and garlic and cook for half a minute more – keep stirring
7. Remove the Brussel sprouts from the heat and drain
8. Serve the sprouts in serving plates

9. Heat up the ground beef, seasoning with the chili powder, salt, and pepper until brown
10. Add the tomato paste to the beef pan and cook for a further 3 minutes
11. Add the sour cream and stir in, cooking until beginning to bubble
12. Serve the mixture over the sprouts

Tips & Tricks/Did You Know?

This particular dish is ideal for a hearty evening meal, and is a great twist on the classic stroganoff recipe. By using Brussel sprouts you are getting your serving of vitamins, and the luxurious taste of the cream and beef together will certainly have you wanting to cook it again!

Cooking time: 10 minutes

Recipe makes 1 serving

Total carbs per serving 3.6g

Ingredients

- 1 Bratwurst, around 3 oz in weight
- Canned sauerkraut, 0.5 cup

Method

1. Preheat a grill over high heat.
2. Grill the bratwurst until browned all over, turning regularly
3. Alternatively, you can microwave the bratwurst for 1-2 minutes
4. Remove the sauerkraut from the can and heat up in your microwave oven
5. Serve together whilst warm

Tips & Tricks/Did You Know?

This particular dish is a popular German favorite, whilst also being filling and nutritious for the first phase of the Atkins Diet. You can easily find both Ingredients in supermarkets, and this dish is also a good source of protein, containing 12.3g per serving.

Cooking time: 10 minutes

Recipe makes 8 servings

Total carbs per serving 3.5g

Ingredients

- Pumpkin, 1lb
- Shallots, chopped, 0.25 cup
- Unsalted butter, 1 tablespoon
- Vegetable broth, 0.25 cup
- Sugar free syrup, 1/16 cup
- Ground sage, 0.25 teaspoon

Method

1. Over high heat, melt the butter in a skillet pan
2. Cut the pumpkin into chunks, around ¾"
3. Add the pumpkin and the shallots to the pan
4. Season with salt and black pepper
5. Cook until the pumpkin has browned and the shallots are clear, this should take just over 5 minutes
6. Turn down the heat and add the vegetable broth
7. Cover the pan and simmer for 10 minutes, or until the pumpkin is tender
8. Add the maple syrup and the sage, stirring everything together
9. Serve!

Tips & Tricks/Did You Know?

To give extra taste and luxury to this particular recipe, use fresh sage, rather than anything else. Around 7/8 leaves will be enough.

Cooking time: 95 minutes

Recipe makes 8 servings

Total carbs per serving 4.7g

Ingredients

- Bacon, 4oz
- Half an onion, sliced
- 6 eggs
- Heavy cream, 0.75 cup

- Broccoli or spinach, 10oz each
- Shredded Swiss cheese, 0.5lb
- Salt, 0.5 teaspoon
- Pepper 0.25 teaspoon

Method

1. Preheat the oven to 180°C
2. Take a 10" quiche pan or a 9" deep pan, butter it to avoid sticking
3. In a skillet pan, cook the bacon until crispy
4. Chop once cooked
5. Remove the oil from the bacon pan, keeping 1 tablespoon of it aside
6. Add the onions to the pan and cook for around 5 minutes, combining with the bacon oil
7. Combine the eggs, cream, broccoli, cheese, salt, and pepper in a large bowl
8. Stir in the bacon and onion
9. Pour the whole mixture into the oiled pan
10.   Bake in the oven for around 1 hour and 15 minutes, until cooked
11.   Allow to cool before cutting into slices

Tips & Tricks/Did You Know?

This is a great recipe for preparing ahead, e.g. for work lunches or even party food. Keep your quiche chilled in the fridge, allowing it to totally cook beforehand, and whip it out when you want to pack your lunch, or you need a snack!

Cooking time: 45 minutes

Recipe makes 2 servings

Total carbs per serving 9.7g

Ingredients

- Half a lemon
- 1 medium young green onion
- 1 head of Romaine or cos lettuce
- 2 medium celery stalks
- 1 red sweet pepper
- 1 tomato, medium
- 1 egg
- Apple cider vinegar, 5 1/3 tablespoons

- Celery salt, 1/8 teaspoons
- Cayenne pepper, 1/8 teaspoons
- Chicken thighs with bone removed, x 2
- Mayonnaise, 0.25 cup
- Sour cream, 2 tablespoons
- Blue cheese 2 or 3 oz
- Garlic powder 1/8 teaspoons
- Salt, 1/3 teaspoons
- Black pepper, ¼ teaspoons

Method

1. Preheat the oven to 230°C
2. Squeeze the juice from the lemon in a bowl
3. Chop up the greens finely and add them to the bowl
4. Add the mayonnaise, sour cream, blue cheese, and garlic powder, stirring to combine together
5. Cut up the lettuce and add to the dressing
6. Cut the celery into small pieces and add to the dressing also
7. Cut up the bell pepper and tomato and add to the bowl
8. Put the bowl in the fridge
9. Beat the eggs together and add the apple cider vinegar black pepper, salt, celery salt, and cayenne pepper – stir together well

10.   Add the chicken to the marinade and bake for 20 minutes, turning and re-brushing a few times. The chicken is cooked when it is crispy
11.   Cut up the chicken and set aside
12.   Take the salad from the fridge and toss
13.   Add the chicken and serve

Tips & Tricks/Did You Know?

If you love chicken Caesar salad, this is actually a good alternative twist for the first phase of your Atkins journey, whilst having plenty of spicy kick! This works well as a lunchtime treat.

Cooking time: 15 minutes

Recipe makes 8 servings

Total carbs per serving 5.4g

Ingredients

- Whole grain soy flour, 1 cup
- Sugar substitute sweetener, 2 tablespoons
- Cinnamon, 2 teaspoons
- Baking powder, 3 teaspoons
- Baking soda, 0.5 teaspoons

- Buttermilk, 0.75 cup
- Unsalted butter, 6 tablespoons
- 3 large eggs
- Sugar free vanilla syrup, 1.5oz
- Tap water, 0.5 cup
- Cooking spray

Method

1. Heat up the waffle pan
2. Add together the soy flour, sugar substitute, cinnamon, baking powder, and soda
3. Add the buttermilk, butter, eggs, and syrup to the mixture and stir well
4. Add the cold water gradually to the mixture, 1 tablespoon at a time; the batter should resemble a pancake batter
5. Spray the waffle pan with cooking spray
6. Add the batter to the waffle pan and cook until crispy and brown
7. Repeat the process until the batter has gone

Tips & Tricks/Did You Know?

This American style breakfast treat gives you a 6.9g boost of protein to start your day. You might think that finding the buttermilk could be difficult, but check your supermarket shelves and you will surely find it! You will need a waffle pan for this particular recipe.

Cooking time: 10 minutes

Recipe makes 4 servings

Total carbs per serving 2.3g

Ingredients

- Brussel sprouts, 2 cups
- Unsalted butter, 2 tablespoons

Method

1. Trim the Brussel sprouts and cut them into halves
2. Salt and boil water and cook the sprouts for around 8 minutes, until they are tender
3. Drain the sprouts
4. Melt the butter over medium heat
5. Add the sprouts and toss, ensuring they are fully coated
6. Season with salt and pepper

Tips & Tricks/Did You Know?

Adding nutmeg to the sprouts gives the dish a different kind of taste. If you're not a big fan of sprouts, try them this way, you will be converted!

Cooking time: 15 minutes

Recipe makes 1 servings

Total carbs per serving 6.8g

Ingredients

- Chopped onions, 1/3 cup
- Extra virgin olive oil, 1 tablespoon
- Shredded cheddar cheese, 0.5 cup
- 2 eggs
- 1 sliced scallion

Method

1. Sauté the onions in olive oil until translucent
2. Remove from the pan and set aside
3. Beat the eggs and add to the same pan
4. Cook until they begin to bubble, before flipping over
5. Add the cheese, onions and scallions to this side and cook for a further minute
6. Fold the omelette in half and cook for a further minute
7. Season to taste

Tips & Tricks/Did You Know?

The omelet is a classic breakfast dish, but can actually be enjoyed at any time of the day. The great thing about this particular dish is that because of the eggs and cheese content, it gives you a big protein hit to start your day, if you choose it for breakfast.

ARTICHOKES WITH LEMON BUTTER

Cooking time: 25 minutes

Recipe makes 4 servings

Total carbs per serving 9.9g

Ingredients

- Medium artichokes, x 4
- Lemons x 4
- Coriander seed, 2 tablespoons

- Salt, 2 tablespoons
- Unsalted butter, 0.5 cup

Method

1. Bring some water to a boil
2. Trim and cut the artichokes and boil
3. Cut 3 lemons in halves and squeeze out the juice into some water
4. Add the rest of the lemon halves, coriander seeds, and the salt
5. Place the artichokes into the liquid and cover it over to stop the artichokes from lifting and floating
6. Boil for 15 minutes
7. Remove and drain the water
8. In a small bowl, melt the butter and mix in the juice of the remaining lemon, adding salt and pepper
9. Serve

Tips & Tricks/Did You Know?

This quick and easy dish can be a snack or a meal, the choice is yours! Whatever you choose, you get a 4.8g hit of protein from chowing down.

Cooking time: 40 minutes

Recipe makes 9 servings

Total carbs per serving 3.8g

Ingredients

- Whole grain soy flour, 0.5 cup
- Wheat gluten, 2oz
- 3 large eggs
- Whole milk, 1 cup
- Salt, 1 teaspoon
- Canola vegetable oil, 1/3 cup
- Baking powder, 1 teaspoon

Method

1. Preheat the oven to 230°C
2. In a small bowl, whisk together the soy flour, gluten, eggs, milk, and salt, until well combined
3. Prepare a square baking dish with oil
4. Place the dish or tray into the oven for 5 minutes to heat up
5. Add the batter evenly to the dish or tray
6. Bake for 15 minutes
7. Turn the oven down to 170°C and continue to bake for another 15-20 minutes, until the pudding is browned
8. Serve hot

Tips & Tricks/Did You Know?

The Yorkshire pudding is an iconic food type which is often served with Sunday roasts. As you can see, you don't need to sacrifice your Sunday meal for your diet, provided you keep an eye on the carb intake of the rest of your roast Ingredients. The pudding itself will give you 9.2g of your protein hit.

Cooking time: 50 minutes

Recipe makes 10 servings

Total carbs per serving 4.8g

Ingredients

- 2 eggs
- Unsalted butter, 0.75 cup
- Sugar substitute, 1/3 cup
- Heavy cream, 2 tablespoons
- Tap water, 1 fluid oz
- Lemon juice, 0.5 teaspoon
- Vanilla extract, 1 teaspoon

- Pure almond extract, 2 teaspoons
- Almond meal flour, 2.5 cups
- Baking powder, 0.5 teaspoons
- Salt, 0.5 teaspoons
- Sugar free red raspberry preserve, 3 1/3 tablespoons

Method

1. Preheat the oven to 230°C
2. In a muffin pan, place muffin cups
3. Beat the egg yolks in a small pan, adding a ¼ cup of sugar substitute, the butter, cream, water, lemon juice and extracts until combined
4. In another bowl, beat the egg whites until they are frothy
5. Add the rest of the sugar substitute and beat until soft peaks have formed
6. Fold the egg whites into the mixture carefully
7. In another bowl still, combine the almond meal, baking powder, and the salt
8. Fold this into the egg mixture and divide between the muffin cups
9. Drop 1 teaspoon of jam into the center of each mixture
10. Bake for half an hour
11. Cool for 20 minutes

Tips & Tricks/Did You Know?

These tasty snacks can be kept for other days, provided you keep them in an airtight container once they have been cooled. They will keep for up to one week.

Cooking time: 30 minutes

Recipe makes 4 servings

Total carbs per serving 2.5g

Ingredients

- Ground beef, 6 oz
- Green chili peppers, 0.5 cup
- Garlic powder, 0.25 teaspoon
- Chili powder, 1 teaspoon
- Cumin, 0.25 teaspoon
- Oregano, 0.25 teaspoon
- Salt, 0.25 teaspoon

- Black pepper, 0.25 teaspoon
- Canadian bacon, 4 slices
- 4 eggs
- Shredded cheddar cheese, 0.5 cup
- Cilantro, 4 pieces

Method

1. Grease a skillet pan and place over medium heat
2. Add the beef and brown it
3. Add the chilies, garlic, chili powder, cumin, oregano, salt, and pepper. Cook for around 10 minutes
4. Add the bacon over the top of the beef for a few minutes
5. Remove the pan from the heat
6. Heat up another skillet pan with oil and scramble the eggs to your liking
7. To serve, add a piece of bacon to each plate, add some of the beef, and some of the eggs
8. Sprinkle cheese and cilantro on top of the dish

Tips & Tricks/Did You Know?

You can mix this recipe up a little if you prefer a different type of egg, so if you like fried or poached eggs, simply change the way you cook the eggs accordingly.

Cooking time: 1 hour

Recipe makes 4 servings

Total carbs per serving 7g

Ingredients

- Ground cumin, 2 tablespoons
- Minced garlic, 3 cloves
- Lime juice, 3 tablespoons
- Black pepper, 1 teaspoon
- Salt, 0.5 teaspoon
- 1 – 1.5lbs steak

- 1 chopped tomato
- Mild green chilies, 1 can drained
- 2 sliced scallions
- Chili powder, 0.5 teaspoon

Method

1. Preheat the grill and spray your cooking plate with cooking oil or spray
2. Cook the cumin for around 3 minutes in the skillet
3. Placed the cooked cumin in a small bowl
4. Add the garlic, 2 tablespoons of lime juice, some black pepper, and ¼ teaspoons of salt. Mix together well
5. Wash the steak and rub the cumin mixture all over
6. Grill the steak and cook to your liking
7. Mix together the tomato, chilies, scallions, chili powder, and some lime juice and salt
8. Slice the steak and serve with salsa

Tips & Tricks/Did You Know?

Flank steak or top round steak works best for this type of recipe, however if you prefer a different cut you can easily adapt it to your liking.

Cooking time: 20 minutes

Recipe makes 1 serving

Total carbs per serving 5.1g

Ingredients

- Sweet red peppers, 1 or 2
- 2 eggs
- Canola vegetable oil, 1 teaspoon
- Shredded mozzarella cheese, 0.25 cup

Method

1. Cut the bell pepper in the middle and cut into rings, removing the seeds
2. Add the rings to the sauté pan over medium heat
3. Add one egg to each ring and cook until done to your liking
4. Add cheese on top of the eggs
5. Cover the pan and cook for a further minute
6. Season with salt and pepper

Tips & Tricks/Did You Know?

By eating this particular recipe you are getting a big intake of antioxidants, so make sure you pick the brightest peppers you can find, to get the most benefit for your health.

BEEF BURGER WITH FETA AND TOMATO

Cooking time: 22 minutes

Recipe makes 4 servings

Total carbs per serving 1.3g

Ingredients

- Ground beef, 1lb
- Spring onion or scallions, one
- Baby spinach, 0.5 cup
- Sliced or chopped tomatoes, 0.25 cup
- Crumbled feta cheese, 0.25 cup
- Fresh dill, 1.5 teaspoons
- Salt, 0.5 teaspoon
- Black pepper, 0.5 teaspoon

Method

1. In a large bowl, mix together with beef, spring onion/scallion, tomato, feta, dill, salt and pepper
2. Split the mixture into four and form burgers
3. Heat a grill or pan over medium heat
4. Cook the burgers on each side for around 6 minutes, or a little more if you prefer well-done burgers

Tips & Tricks/Did You Know?

This particular dish will give you a large hit of your daily protein amount, at 24.3g. You can add in low carb bread if you like a traditional burger, but remember to add the carb amount to your daily allowance.

Cooking time: 15 minutes

Recipe makes 4 servings

Total carbs per serving 4.4g

Ingredients

- Vanilla whey protein, 2 oz
- Almond meal flour, 0.25 cup
- Whole grain soy flour, 3 tablespoons

- Baking powder, 1 teaspoon
- 3 eggs
- Creamed cottage cheese, 1/3 cup

Method

1. In a large bowl, mix together the why protein, almond meal flour, soy flour and baking powder until well combined
2. In another bowl, whisk up the eggs and add the cottage cheese
3. Over medium heat, heat a griddle pan and add canola oil or butter to grease
4. Drop the batter into the pan, around ¼ cup for each one
5. The batter will bubble up and this is when you should turn the pancake over and cook until it is firm to touch
6. Repeat the process until the batter is gone

Tips & Tricks/Did You Know?

You can make this recipe even more delicious by serving it with pancake syrup, the sugar free variety, or you can add toasted almonds – be careful of the extra carb content however, and add this to your consideration.

Cooking time: 35 minutes

Recipe makes 6 servings

Total carbs per serving 5.9g

Ingredients

- Bacon, 6 medium slices
- Unsalted butter, 3 tablespoons
- 2 leeks
- Mushrooms, 2 cups

- Cauliflower, 1.5 cups
- Chicken broth, 2 x 14.5oz cans
- Water, 0.5 cup
- Blue cheese, 2.5oz

Method

1. Cut the bacon into small strips
2. Cook the bacon by frying over medium heat in a skillet pan, make sure they are crispy
3. Pat the bacon dry by placing on a kitchen roll paper and blotting
4. Wait until the bacon is cool and then crumble it up
5. In a large pot, melt the button over medium heat
6. Add the mushrooms and cauliflower to the pot, cook for 5 minutes and stir from time to time
7. Add the chicken, broth, and water to the pan
8. Lower the heat and simmer for 10 minutes
9. Puree the soup using a blender or a food processor in batches
10. Add each batch of soup back to the pot
11. Add the cheese to the last batch before pureeing
12. Reheat if needed
13. Crumble the bacon over the top before serving

Tips & Tricks/Did You Know?

If you're not a fan of blue cheese, you can add Roquefort as an alternative.

Cooking time: 1 hour

Recipe makes 4 servings

Total carbs per serving 10g

Ingredients

- Olive oil, 2 tablespoons
- Red bell pepper, half, chopped
- Minced garlic, 6 cloves
- Greens, this can be frozen, and two different types at 10oz each
- Water, 1 cup

- Cider vinegar, 2 tablespoons
- Salt, ¼ teaspoon
- Pork tenderloin, 1lb, cut finely
- 2 Serrano peppers chopped finely
- Black pepper, 1 teaspoon

Method

1. Over medium heat, warm up 2 tablespoons of oil
2. Add the pepper and garlic to the pan and cook until slightly brown
3. Chop the greens
4. Add the greens and the water to the pan and bring it to a boil before reducing the heat and covering the pan
5. Simmer for 20 minutes, remember to stir occasionally
6. Add the vinegar and stir, add the salt and stir
7. Remove the skillet from the heat
8. In a bowl, mix up the pork strips, red peppers, and black pepper
9. Heat another 1 tablespoon of oil in a separate skillet
10. Add the pork and cook until thoroughly heated, around 3-5 minutes
11. Serve the pork over the greens

Tips & Tricks/Did You Know?

If you don't like the heat of a serrano pepper, you can substitute this with a regular red pepper, however go for the brightest possible, to get the best amount of antioxidants into your diet. If you are using serrano peppers, do remember that you should be wearing rubber gloves when handling them, and certainly don't forget to wash your hands afterward!

Cooking time: 10 minutes

Recipe makes 1 serving

Total carbs per serving 5.3g

Ingredients

- Chopped cucumber, 0.5 cup
- Lemon juice, 2 tablespoons
- Blueberries, 1 oz
- Sweetener, 0.5 teaspoons
- Rosemary, 1 teaspoon
- Ice cubes, x4
- Club soda, 4 oz

Method

1. Chop up the cucumber
2. Blend 0.5 cup of cucumber
3. Add the lemon juice, blueberries and sugar substitute
4. Blend together thoroughly
5. Add the rosemary to the mixture and pulse the blender a couple of times
6. Strain the mixture out thoroughly
7. You can throw away the pulp
8. To the glass add the ice, and then add the club soda (and gin if required)
9. Stir and enjoy!

Tips & Tricks/Did You Know?

You can make this particular drink alcoholic if you want to, by adding 1 fluid oz of gin to the mixture and knocking off 1 oz of club soda.

Cooking time: 15 minutes

Recipe makes 4 servings

Total carbs per serving 3.3g

Ingredients

- Spring onions or scallions, x 4
- Tap water, 1 fluid oz
- Sugar substitute, 1 teaspoon
- Canola vegetable oil, 1 tablespoon
- Sesame oil, 1 teaspoon
- Chinese cabbage, either Bok-Choy or Pak-Choi works well, 8 heads

- Garlic, 1.5 teaspoons
- Red pepper, crushed, 1/8 teaspoons
- Peanuts in the shell, 1 cup
- Tamari soybean sauce, 2 tablespoons

Method

1. Take a small bowl and combine together the tamari, water, and sugar substitute
2. Heat up a wok or skillet pan with the canola and sesame oils
3. When the pan is hot, add the Chinese cabbage, garlic, soy sauce and pepper
4. Stir fry for around 3 minutes
5. Stir in the peanuts to serve

Tips & Tricks/Did You Know?

Chinese cabbage has a distinct taste which certainly has the oriental about it. This recipe is not at all tasteless as the name would perhaps suggest, and it certainly goes very well on its own; having said that, if you add the extra carbs, why not throw in some chicken and give yourself a real feast?

Cooking time: 20 minutes

Recipe makes 4 servings

Total carbs per serving 5.1g

Ingredients

- Light olive oil, 2 tablespoons
- Chopped onions, 2 tablespoons
- Pork chops, 16oz
- Monterey Jack cheese, 1oz
- Salsa verde, 0.25 cup

- Jalapeno pepper, x 1
- Coriander, 0.25 cup
- Black pepper, 1 teaspoon
- Salt 0.25 teaspoon
- Low carb tortilla x 1

Method

1. Preheat the oven to 230°C
2. Heat 1 tablespoon of oil in a large pan
3. Add the chopped onion and cook for 5 minutes
4. Add the onion to a bowl and add the pork, cheese, salsa, jalapeno, cilantro, pepper, and salt
5. Mix up the mixture well
6. Take the tortilla and brush one side with the rest of the oil
7. Smooth some of the mixture over the side of the tortilla that hasn't been oiled
8. Fold in half
9. Bake in the oven for 5 minutes, until golden and crispy

Tips & Tricks/Did You Know?

This particular dish is ideal for the second phase, but make sure you check the label of the tortillas, to make sure they don't contain more than 3g of carbs each. You can serve these delicious quesadillas, with sour cream if you like.

BREAKFAST MEXI PEPPERS

Cooking time: 1 hour

Recipe makes 4 servings

Total carbs per serving 5.3g

Ingredients

- Pork and beef chorizo, 4 oz
- Ground beef, 4 oz
- Chopped onions, 0.5 cup
- Shredded cheddar cheese, 0.25 cup
- 3 legs
- Sweet red peppers, x 2

Method

1. Preheat the oven to 200°C
2. Line a baking tray with foil
3. Cook the chorizo until brown, make sure you drain off the fat
4. Into a small mixing bowl combine the chorizo and ground beef
5. Add the onion, cheese, and eggs
6. Cut the peppers in half and remove the seeds
7. Fill each of the peppers with the mixture
8. Bake in the oven for half an hour

Tips & Tricks/Did You Know?

This morning snack is certainly going to keep you full until lunchtime, as it is packed with 21.3g of protein, meaning you're not likely to feel hungry or want to snack mid-morning. Again, go for the reddest pepper you can find, as this will have more vitamins.

Cooking time: 15 minutes

Recipe makes 4 servings

Total carbs per serving 3.5g

Ingredients

- Celery, 1 medium
- Extra virgin olive oil, 2 tablespoons
- Half a medium carrot
- Garlic, 1 teaspoon
- Parsley, 2 tablespoons
- Chicken broth, 0.5 cup
- Red wine, 4 fluid oz

- Cooked chicken thighs, boneless, 32oz
- 1 onion
- Bay leaf, 0.5 teaspoon, crumbled
- Cooked ham, fresh, boneless, 2oz

Method

1. Over medium heat, add oil to a large skillet
2. Add the onion, carrot and celery, cooking until soft
3. Add the ham and garlic, cooking for a further 2 minutes
4. Add the mixture to a separate bowl
5. Cook the chicken thighs on all sides until brown
6. Add the wine, broth, and bay leaf to the pan and reduce the heat down to medium
7. Cook for half an hour, until the chicken is cooked and liquid is reduced
8. Add the vegetables and ham back to the pan
9. Mix everything up and heat for a further 5 minutes

Tips & Tricks/Did You Know?

Red table wine works best for this particular recipe, and this also doesn't need to be the most expensive brand to add more taste. You can also make this recipe in the first phase, if you take out the carrot.

Cooking time: 5 minutes

Recipe makes 1 serving

Total carbs per serving 17g

Ingredients

- Plain yogurt, 0.5 cup
- Pineapple, 2.5 oz

- Whole almonds, x 20
- Pure almond milk, 0.5 cup

Method:

1. Add all Ingredients to a blender
2. Combine until smooth
3. Serve immediately

Tips & Tricks/Did You Know?

This particular drink is very high in carbs, so it should be kept into moderation and only consumed occasionally. The third phase introduces more in the way of exotic fruits, but pineapple does have many weight loss busting elements, so make sure you have this occasionally, however only ever use fresh, canned is not as good.

Cooking time: 45 minutes

Recipe makes 6 servings

Total carbs per serving 6.3g

Ingredients

- Ground beef, 1.5lbs
- Chopped onions, 0.25 cup
- Green pepper (sweeter the better), chopped, 0.25 cup
- Canned tomato sauce, 15oz
- Tomato paste, 4 tablespoons
- Sugar substitute, 3 teaspoons
- Shredded Romaine lettuce, 6 cups
- Cheddar cheese, 6oz

Method

1. Over medium heat, brown the beef
2. Add the onions and peppers towards the end of the beef cooking
3. Add the tomato sauce, tomato paste, and sugar substitute, salt, and pepper.
4. Turn the heat down to low and simmer for around half an hour.
5. Once cooked, serve straight away over Romaine with cheddar sprinkled on top.

Tips & Tricks/Did You Know?

You can mix this recipe up and make it a more Mexican style by adding cayenne pepper to the beef, and you could even use it in wraps for a tortilla-style; just remember to add the extra carbs for the wrap.

Cooking time: 45 minutes

Recipe makes 6 servings

Total carbs per serving 1.9g

Ingredients

- Cider vinegar, 1 cup
- Canola vegetable oil, 0.5 cup
- Black pepper, 0.5 teaspoon
- Garlic powder, 0.5 teaspoon
- Salt, 1 teaspoon
- Celery salt, 0.25 teaspoon
- Cayenne pepper, 1/8 teaspoon

- Chicken wings, 32oz
- 1 egg
- Mayonnaise, 1 cup
- Sour cream, 0.5 cup
- Spring onions or 1 scallion
- Blue cheese, 1/3 cup
- Lemon juice, 0.5 fluid oz

Method

1. Preheat the oven to 230°C
2. Into a medium bowl, beat the egg and add some vinegar, salt, oil, pepper, garlic powder, celery salt, and cayenne. Stir well
3. Dip the chicken into the marinade and place on a baking tray
4. Bake in the oven for half an hour, turning regularly
5. You may need to re-brush with the marinade occasionally
6. Cook until the wings are crispy and cooked through
7. Into another bowl, mix the mayonnaise, sour cream, cheese, scallion/spring onion, lemon juice, and garlic
8. Serve the chicken whilst hot with the dipping sauce in a separate pot

Tips & Tricks/Did You Know?

If cayenne pepper is a little too spicy for you, you can replace this with a milder red pepper, and if you don't like blue cheese, replace it with Roquefort, for a creamier taste to this classic dish.

BAKED BRIE WITH SUN-DRIED TOMATOES AND PINE NUTS

Cooking time: 15 minutes

Recipe makes 6 servings

Total carbs per serving 0.5g

Ingredients

- Brie cheese, 8 oz
- Chopped sun-dried tomatoes, 1 tablespoon
- Parsley, 1 tablespoon
- Dried pine nuts, 0.5 oz

Method

1. Preheat the oven to 230°C
2. Trim the cheese to get rid of any rind.
3. Find a pie plate or something alternative and put the cheese into it.
4. In a bowl combine the sun-dried tomatoes and the parsley
5. Spread the mixture over the cheese evenly
6. Sprinkle the pine nuts over the top
7. Place in the oven for 10 minutes.

Tips & Tricks/Did You Know?

This dish is a fantastic party food suggestion as well as a meal or snack in itself – almost like a fondue, you can add dipping aids, such as low carb bread or tortillas, provided you factor in the extra carbs for your daily intake.

GRILLED TOFU WITH PEANUT SAUCE

Cooking time: 30 minutes

Recipe makes 4 servings

Total carbs per serving 10g

Ingredients

- 2 x tofu packages, 14 oz
- Canola oil, 2 tablespoons for tofu, and 3 tablespoons for sauce
- Salt, 0.25 teaspoon
- Ground black pepper, 0.25 teaspoon
- Tamarind paste, 1 tablespoon
- Minced garlic, 1 tablespoon
- Minced shallot, 1 tablespoon
- Chili paste, 1 teaspoon
- Chopped peanuts, 0.25 cup
- Peanut butter, 2 tablespoons
- Unsweetened coconut milk, 1/3 cup
- Cilantro, chopped, 2 tablespoons

Method

1. Take each tofu pack and cut each into four blocks
2. Take 2 tablespoons of canola oil and rub the tofu with it, add salt and pepper to season
3. Add the tamarind paste into 1/3 cup of water and dissolve
4. Heat 3 tablespoons of canola oil
5. Add the garlic and shallots to the pan, cooked for 1 minute
6. Add the chili paste and peanuts, stir constantly
7. Add the peanut butter and dissolved tamarind, then the coconut milk
8. Cover the mixture and keep warm
9. Preheat the grill over low heat
10. Grill the tofu for 10 seconds on each side
11. Serve by pouring the sauce over each block of tofu, and sprinkle with cilantro

Smooth peanut butter works best for this recipe, however if you are struggling to find it, or you prefer a different variety you can add this, simply add the extra carb intake (if any) to the total.

Cooking time: 135 minutes

Recipe makes 10 servings

Total carbs per serving 2.4g

Ingredients

- Dried Porcini mushrooms, 15 pieces
- Extra virgin olive oil, 1 tablespoon
- Beef brisket, 4 lbs
- Onion x 2
- Garlic, 1.5 teaspoons
- Beef broth, 1 can/14oz
- Crumbled Bay leaf, 1 teaspoon
- Salt, 0.5 teaspoon
- Black pepper, 0.25 teaspoon

Method

1. Into a small bowl add the mushrooms and 0.75 cups of water
2. Microwave the mixture on high until the water is boiling
3. Allow to cool
4. Over a medium heat, warm up the oil
5. Take the brisket and warm it on one side, turn over and add the onions
6. Add the garlic when the onions are brown, cook for a further one minute
7. Take the mushrooms from the liquid (keep the liquid to one side)
8. Rinse the mushrooms and chop roughly
9. Place the mushrooms to the brisket
10. Strain the reserved liquid from the mushrooms and add to the brisket mixture
11. Add the broth, Bay leaf, salt and pepper
12. Cover the mixture and reduce the heat down to low
13. Cook for 2-2.5 hours and then remove the brisket
14. Turn the heat up and cook until the juices are thickened
15. Cut the brisket into slices and serve with the liquid mixture

If you're looking for a winter warmer, this dish works fantastic as an alternative to old fashioned stews. You will also get a huge hit of protein too, which we know is very important on the Atkins diet, no matter what stage you are in.

SPICY HUMMUS

Cooking time: 15 minutes

Recipe makes 16 servings

Total carbs per serving 11g

Ingredients

- Chickpeas, 2 cups (drained and rinsed)
- Lime juice, 6 tablespoons
- Extra virgin olive oil, 0.25 cup
- Sesame paste, 0.25 cup
- Roasted red pepper in a jar, x1
- Minced garlic, 2 cloves
- Ground cumin, 2 teaspoons
- Salt, 1 teaspoon
- Cayenne pepper, 0.5 teaspoon
- Water, 0.5 cup

Method

1. Place the chickpeas, lime juice, olive oil, sesame paste, red pepper, garlic, cumin, salt, and cayenne into a food processer until it forms a smooth paste in consistency
2. Whilst you are pureeing, pour the water very slowly into the tube until it is as thick or thin as you like
3. Serve or store

Tips & Tricks/Did You Know?

Although you can easily buy hummus in the supermarket, it can be quite expensive, so it is much more cost effective, and probably healthier to make your own. If you want to give your hummus a spicy kick, simply add more cayenne pepper. You can store this recipe for up to 2 days in the fridge.

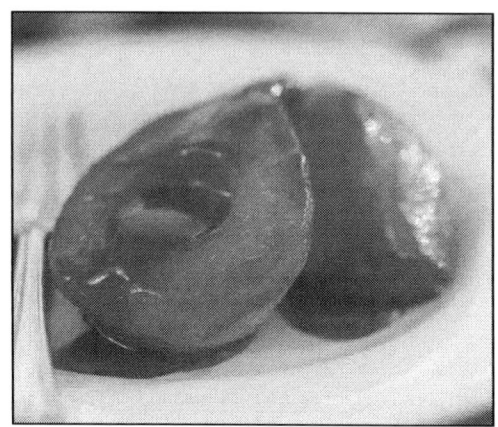

Cooking time: 10 minutes

Recipe makes 8 servings

Total carbs per serving 7.6g

Ingredients

- Butter, 2 tablespoons
- Xylitol, 2 tablespoons
- Ground cardamom, 0.25 teaspoon
- Pears, x 2
- 3 eggs

- 2 egg yolks
- Heavy cream, 2 cups
- Low calorie maple syrup (sugar free) 1/8 cups
- Rum, 0.5 fluid oz
- Vanilla extract, 1 teaspoon

Method

1. Preheat the oven to 190°C
2. Warm up the butter, xylitol, and the cardamom over a medium to high heat
3. Slice up the pears into wedges, around 0.5" each
4. Add the pears once the butter is melted and leave for 4 minutes on each side
5. Place the pears into a casserole dish or high sided plate
6. Pour 2 tablespoons of the maple syrup over the pears
7. Into a small bowl, mix up the eggs, yolks, heavy cream, syrup, rum, and vanilla
8. Pour over the pears
9. Bake in the oven for around 20 minutes
10.   Brush the top of the dish with the rest of the syrup

Tips & Tricks/Did You Know?

You can omit the rum if you want to go for a non-alcoholic option to this dish.

Cooking time: 30 minutes

Recipe makes 4 servings

Total carbs per serving 10g

Ingredients

- Unsalted butter, 1 teaspoon
- 2 eggs
- Heavy cream, 2 tablespoons
- Grated parmesan cheese, 2 tablespoons

Method

1. Preheat the oven to 190°C
2. Find an oven safe dish and melt the butter, coating the inside of the dish
3. Into a small bowl, mix together the eggs and cream
4. Add the cheese, ground black pepper, and salt, mix together
5. Bake in the oven for 10 minutes

Tips & Tricks/Did You Know?

This particular dish is actually suitable for all phases, but is a delicious recipe to try in phase 3, if you are running low on your carb intake for that particular meal. You could of course add low carb bread if you have a few extra carbs spare.

Cooking time: 25 minutes

Recipe makes 10 servings

Total carbs per serving 3.7g

Ingredients

- Extra virgin olive oil, 1 tablespoon
- Chopped onions, 0.25 cup
- Tomato paste, 2 tablespoons
- Chili powder, 1 teaspoon
- Cumin, 1 teaspoon
- Garlic powder, 0.75 teaspoon
- Yellow mustard seed, 0.75 teaspoon
- Ground allspice, 0.75 teaspoon
- Cayenne pepper, 1/8 teaspoon
- Ketchup, unsweetened, 1.5 cups
- Cider vinegar, 1 tablespoon
- Worcestershire sauce, 2/3 tablespoons
- Sugar substitute, 2 tablespoons
- Instant dry coffee powder, 0.25 teaspoons

Method

1. Over a medium to high heat, warm up the oil
2. Add the onion and cook for around 3 minutes
3. Add the tomato paste, chili, cumin, garlic, mustard, allspice, cayenne pepper and cook for another minute
4. Add the ketchup, vinegar, Worcestershire sauce, sugar substitute, and coffee
5. Simmer the mixture and stir occasionally for around 8 minutes – it should thicken up considerably
6. Serve or wait to cool before storing

Tips & Tricks/Did You Know?

Each particular serving of this sauce works out at a generous 2 tablespoons, which works out your total carb intake for this recipe. If you go over, remember to adjust accordingly; it's very easy to have too much sauce!

QUICK REMINDER OF PHASE 4

Phase 4 is your maintenance phase, and this is where you are going to stay for the rest of your life. Don't panic, it's not as drastic as it sounds! Basically, at this point you are at your goal and you have now recognized your carb intake level, the natural amount you can eat without the scales budging either way. If you do find you are putting weight on, you can drop back down a phase, or even go back to phase 1 if you need to – the Atkins Diet is personal in that way.

- Stick to your personal carb intake level
- Remember to keep your protein up
- Mix and match your food to stop boredom creeping in
- Try and recognize this as a healthy lifestyle, rather than a dietary phase

Cooking time: 30 minutes

Recipe makes 4 servings

Total carbs per serving 5.2g

Ingredients

- Unsalted butter, 2 tablespoons
- Leek x 1
- Asparagus, 0.75lb

- Garlic, 1 teaspoon
- Chicken broth, 14.5 oz
- Heavy cream, 1/3 cup

Method

1. In a large pot, melt the butter, before adding the leeks and cooking for around 3 minutes
2. Add the asparagus and cook for a further minute
3. Add the garlic and cook for half a minute
4. Add the broth and bring the pot to a boil
5. Turn the heat down and simmer for around 10 minutes
6. Add the cream, salt and pepper
7. Blend the soup in a blender or food processor
8. Heat up if required
9. Season to taste

Tips & Tricks/Did You Know?

You can make this soup in batches and keep for a few days, provided you wait for it to cool completely and then store in an airtight container in the fridge.

CHOCOLATE AND HAZELNUT MOUSSE

Cooking time: 3.5 hours

Recipe makes 6 servings

Total carbs per serving 3g

Ingredients

- Low carb chocolate, 4 oz
- Unsalted butter, 4 teaspoons
- Hazelnut syrup (sugar free), 4 teaspoons
- Heavy cream, 1 1/3 cups
- Sugar substitute, 4 teaspoons
- Chopped and toasted hazelnuts, 4 tablespoons
- Fresh raspberries, x6

Method

1. Into a small bowl melt the chocolate, butter, and syrup over low heat
2. Transfer to a bowl and set to one side
3. Add the cream and sugar substitute to another bowl and whip together well
4. Fold 1/3 of the mixture into the chocolate and stir
5. Combine the rest and stir
6. Add the hazelnuts and raspberry as a garnish

Tips & Tricks/Did You Know?

This particular delicious treat will keep for up to 3 hours, but transfer to the fridge if you aren't eating straight away.

Cooking time: 30 minutes

Recipe makes 4 servings

Total carbs per serving 5g

Ingredients

- 2 eggs
- Cauliflower florets, 4 cups
- Almond flour, 4 tablespoons
- Chili powder, 1 teaspoon
- Canola oil

- Fish sauce, 2 teaspoons
- Lime juice, 1 tablespoon
- Scallions, chopped, 1 tablespoon

Method

1. Combine the eggs in a large bowl and toss in the cauliflower florets, coating completely.
2. Place the florets onto a plate
3. Add the almond flour and chili powder, sprinkling over the top
4. Using a wok or high sided frying pan, fill with canola oil and heat to 170°C
5. Fry the florets in the oil
6. Transfer to paper towels to absorb extra oil
7. Drizzle with fish sauce and lime juice
8. Add the chopped scallions as a garnish

Tips & Tricks/Did You Know?

If you're not the biggest cauliflower fan, you can deep fry other vegetables, simply being careful of the carb amount and adjusting the number accordingly. Having said the cauliflower gives 7g of protein.

ASIAN VEGETABLE BOWL

Cooking time: 20 minutes

Recipe makes 6 servings

Total carbs per serving 4.6g

Ingredients

- Spring onions, 3 cups
- Mushrooms, 2 cups
- Tamari soybean sauce, 4 tablespoons
- Ginger, 3 teaspoons
- Garlic, 1 clove
- Serrano pepper, x1

- Sliced red tomato, 1 cup
- Tofu, the firm variety, 6 oz
- Carrot
- Cilantro, 0.5 oz
- Chinese cabbage, shredded, 2 cups
- Chicken broth, 6 cups

Method

1. Heat up the broth and tamari and bring to a boil
2. Turn down the heat and add the Chinese cabbage, mushrooms, ginger, garlic, and chili
3. Simmer for around 5 minutes
4. Add the tomatoes, onions, tofu, and carrot, cook for around 1 minute more
5. Stir in the cilantro and serve

Tips & Tricks/Did You Know?

You can make this particular recipe acceptable for the first phase if you simply take out the carrot. If you are vegetarian, then simply omit the chicken broth and replace it with the vegetable variety.

Cooking time: 5 minutes

Recipe makes 1 serving

Total carbs per serving 8.9g

Ingredients

- Small banana, 1/3
- Coconut cream, 1/3 cup
- Rum, 1 fluid oz
- Ice cubes, x2
- Sweetener, 0.75 teaspoon

Method

1. Combine the banana, coconut, rum, and sugar substitute in a blender, before adding the ice
2. Blend until totally combined
3. Serve in a glass and enjoy!

Tips & Tricks/Did You Know?

You can go for spiced rum if you prefer but do check regarding the carb intake of your particular chosen variety – some do harbor hidden carbs! If you want to go non-alcoholic, simply use rum extract rather than actual rum.

Cooking time: 15 minutes

Recipe makes 1 serving

Total carbs per serving 3g

Ingredients

- Canola oil, 1 teaspoon
- Turkey breakfast sausage, 4 links (cooked)
- Red sweet pepper, 1 quarter
- Green sweet pepper, 1 quarter
- Monterey Jack cheese, 1 oz

Method

1. Over medium heat, add the oil to a skillet pan and heat up
2. You can either crumble the sausage or slice after cooking, but add to the pan and brown for around 3 minutes
3. Add the red and green peppers
4. Cook for a further 5 minutes
5. Sprinkle on the cheese, allowing to melt
6. Serve

Tips & Tricks/Did You Know?

Different types of breakfast sausage work just as well if you don't like turkey, but do check the carb intake amount.

CAJUN PORK CHOPS

Cooking time: 20 minutes

Recipe makes 4 servings

Total carbs per serving 0.7g

Ingredients

- Paprika, 1 tablespoon
- Cumin, 0.5 teaspoon
- Ground sage, 0.5 teaspoon
- Black pepper, 0.5 teaspoon
- Garlic powder, 0.5 teaspoon

- Cayenne pepper, 0.5 teaspoon
- Pork chops, 24oz
- Unsalted butter, 0.5 tablespoons
- Canola oil, 0.5 tablespoons

Method

1. In a bowl, combine all the spices
2. Season the pork chops on both sides
3. Over high heat, melt the butter and oil
4. Cook the chops in the skillet over medium heat for just under 10 minutes, turn halfway through
5. Serve

Tips & Tricks/Did You Know?

If you are running low on carbs on a particular day and you want a hearty, delicious meal, this is a great option, which is extremely low in carb intake, whilst being high in protein.

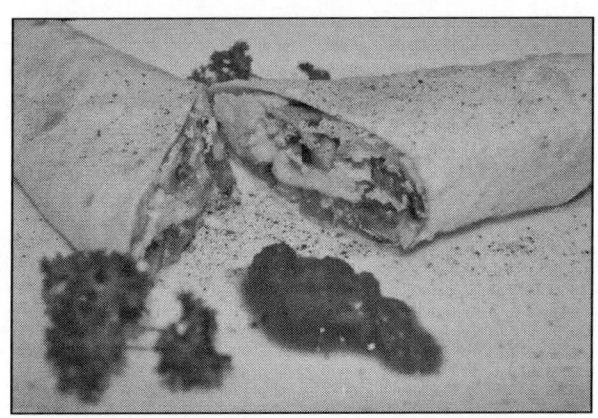

Cooking time: 20 minutes

Recipe makes 2 servings

Total carbs per serving 7.9g

Ingredients

- Salt, 0.5 teaspoon
- Cayenne pepper, 0.25 teaspoon
- Canola oil, 1 tablespoon
- Eggs x 4
- Sweet red peppers, 3 tablespoons

- Spring onions, 2 tablespoons
- Jalapeno pepper, x1
- Low carb tortillas, x2
- Tabasco sauce, 1/8 teaspoon
- Salsa, 2oz

Method

1. Whisk up the eggs, cayenne, and salt
2. Over medium heat, toast the tortillas for a minute, turning and repeating
3. Cook the oil, red pepper, spring onion, and jalapeno until soft, for about 3 minutes
4. Add the eggs and stir, cooking for around 2 minutes more
5. Divide the mixture between the tortillas
6. Season with the tabasco sauce
7. Roll up the tortillas
8. Serve with the salsa and greens

Tips & Tricks/Did You Know?

Be careful of the brand of salsa you use, and always check the label. Every single company makes their product differently and some may have a higher carb content than others – shop around.

Cooking time: 1 hour 20 minutes

Recipe makes 4 servings

Total carbs per serving 4g

Ingredients

- Mashed avocados, 2 cups
- Lime zest, 0.5 teaspoon
- Lime juice, 3 oz
- Powdered xylitol, 0.25 cups
- Stevia crystals, 0.5 teaspoon
- Vanilla extract, 2 teaspoons
- Salt, 1 pinch
- Ground cinnamon, 1 pinch
- Ground nutmeg, 1 pinch
- Almond butter, 2 tablespoons
- Extract (your choice), 0.25 teaspoon
- Strawberries, 0.25 cup

Method

1. In a food processor, place all Ingredients (except strawberries) and combine until creamy
2. Remove from the processor and allow it to rest for around 20 minutes at the very least
3. Add the strawberries as a garnish

Tips & Tricks/Did You Know?

For the best taste, make sure you go for medium ripe avocados; if they are too ripe the taste will be too strong, and if they are under ripe, the taste will be neither here nor there.

Cooking time: 20 minutes

Recipe makes 6 servings

Total carbs per serving 3.8g

Ingredients

- Spring onions, x 3
- Mayonnaise, 4 tablespoons
- Lemon juice, 1 fluid oz
- Sugar substitute, 1 teaspoon
- Ground mustard, 0.5 teaspoon

- Cauliflower head x 1
- Jalapeno pepper x1
- Salt, 1/8 teaspoon
- Black pepper, 1/8 teaspoon

Method

1. Cook the cauliflower first of all in salted water, to your taste
2. Drain and pat dry the cauliflower
3. Mix together the mayonnaise, lemon juice, sugar substitute and mustard, until well combined
4. Add the cauliflower, pepper, and onion
5. Mix together until well coated
6. Add salt and pepper

Tips & Tricks/Did You Know?

For the best flavor, put the dish in the fridge after mixing together and leave for at least half an hour.

Cooking time: 20 minutes

Recipe makes 6 servings

Total carbs per serving 5g

Ingredients

- Feta cheese, cut into chunks, 150 g
- Feta brine, 2 tablespoon
- Fresh lime juice, 3 tablespoons
- Extra virgin olive oil, 4 tablespoons
- Plum tomatoes, 1 cup

- Cucumber, 0.75 cup
- Red onion, 0.5 cup
- Green bell pepper, 0.75 cup
- Black olives, 1/3 cup
- Arugula, 2 cups
- Dried oregano, 2 tablespoons
- Salt, 1 teaspoon

Method

1. Blend up half of the feta cheese, brine, olive oil, and lemon juice in a blender or food processor
2. Mix together the rest of the Ingredients in a bowl (except the arugula)
3. Add the dressing and mix
4. Add the arugula and toss gently

Tips & Tricks/Did You Know?

This particular salad works well as a side salad to a main meal, as it is low in carbs and not the highest in protein either – add a meat dish to up your protein amount.

Cooking time: 15 minutes

Recipe makes 8 servings

Total carbs per serving 1.5g

Ingredients

- Heavy cream, 1 cup
- Roquefort cheese, 0.5 cup (crumbled)
- Jarlsberg cheese, 2 oz
- Grated parmesan cheese, 0.25 cup
- Paprika, 0.5 teaspoon

Method

1. Over low heat, heat up the cream
2. Add the Roquefort until melted
3. Add the Jarlsberg until melted
4. Add the parmesan until melted
5. Add the paprika and continue to cook until hot and smooth, stirring regularly
6. Season with salt and pepper

Tips & Tricks/Did You Know?

If you don't like any of the cheese in this particular recipe, you can substitute them for others, but simply check if there are any additional carbs to take into account for your calculations.

CONCLUSION

This book is designed to give you inspiration and ideas for what you can eat during your time on the Atkins Diet, at each phase. Probably the most daunting thing about starting a diet is 'what am I going to eat?' and worrying about what you are going to miss. The main plus point of the Atkins Diet, aside from the weight loss side of things, is that you can eat many things that you can't eat on a regular diet, and because of that you don't get hungry, and you're not at the mercy of cravings.

For this reason alone, the Atkins Diet is very easy to follow.

If you try even half of the recipes we have talked about in this book, you will see how delicious the Atkins Diet can be, and you will certainly be very full indeed as a result!

Of course, you can modify any of our recipes, provided you take into account the amount of carbohydrates you are taking in, as well as making sure you get your protein allowance per day; this currently stands at 4-6oz per day, depending on your body weight, so check current guidelines to make sure you are getting enough – protein is extremely important.

Give these recipes a try for yourself, and see how easy and delicious the Atkins Diet can be.

YOUR GIFT

I wanted to show my appreciation that you support my work so I've put together a free gift for you.

http://bonusfreebook.org/

Just visit the link above to download it now.

I know you will love this gift.

Thank you for attention!

With love,

John Thornton

Printed in Great Britain
by Amazon